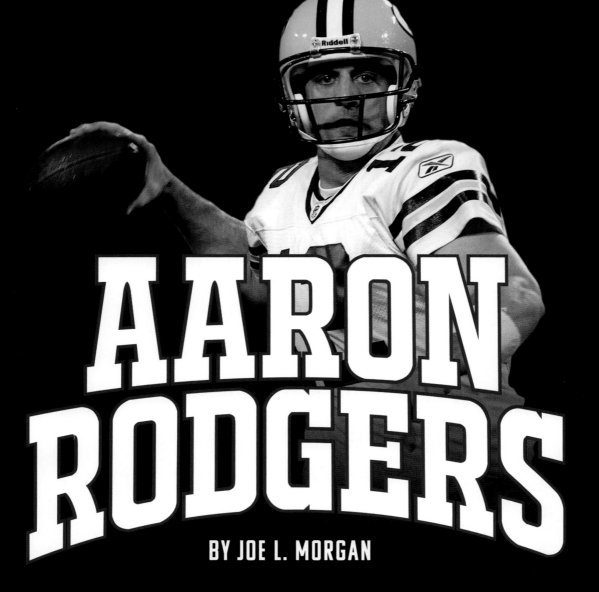

GRIDIRON GREATS
PRO FOOTBALL'S BEST PLAYERS

AARON RODGERS

BY JOE L. MORGAN

GRIDIRON GREATS
PRO FOOTBALL'S BEST PLAYERS

AARON RODGERS

ANTONIO BROWN

DREW BREES

J.J. WATT

JULIO JONES

ROB GRONKOWSKI

RUSSELL WILSON

TOM BRADY

VON MILLER

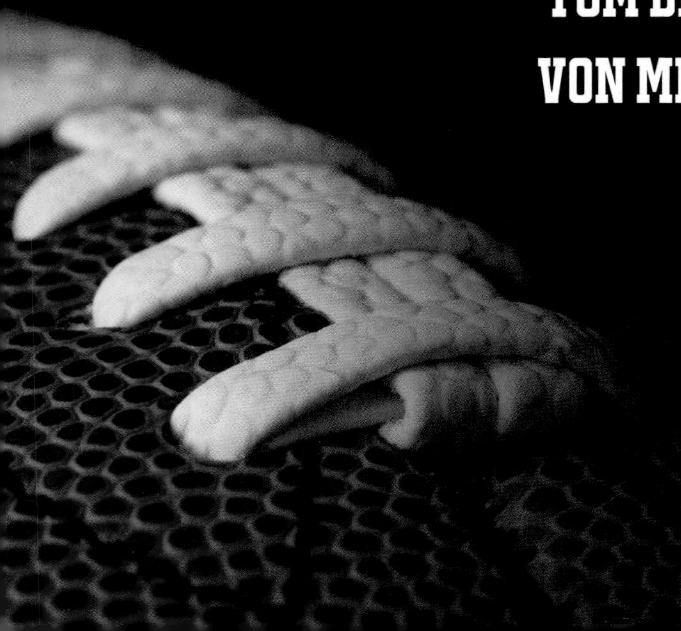

GRIDIRON GREATS
PRO FOOTBALL'S BEST PLAYERS

AARON RODGERS

BY JOE L. MORGAN

MASON CREST

Mason Crest
450 Parkway Drive, Suite D
Broomall, Pennsylvania 19008
(866) MCP-BOOK (toll-free)
www.masoncrest.com

First printing
9 8 7 6 5 4 3 2 1

ISBN (hardback) 978-1-4222-4068-7
ISBN (series) 978-1-4222-4067-0
ISBN (ebook) 978-1-4222-7719-5

Library of Congress Cataloging-in-Publication Data

Names: Morgan, Joe L., author.
Title: Aaron Rodgers / Joe L. Morgan.
Description: Broomall, Pennsylvania : Mason Crest, an imprint of National
   Highlights, Inc., [2018] | Series: Gridiron greats: Pro football's best
   players | Includes webography. | Includes index.
Identifiers: LCCN 2018020753 (print) | LCCN 2018022743 (ebook) | ISBN
   9781422277195 (eBook) | ISBN 9781422240687 (hardback) | ISBN 9781422240670
   (series)
Subjects: LCSH: Rodgers, Aaron, 1983—-Juvenile literature. | Quarterbacks
   (Football)—United States—Biography—Juvenile literature. | Football
   players—United States—Biography—Juvenile literature.
Classification: LCC GV939.R6235 (ebook) | LCC GV939.R6235 M67 2018 (print) |
   DDC 796.332092 [B] —dc23
LC record available at https://lccn.loc.gov/2018020753

NATIONAL
HIGHLIGHTS

Developed and Produced by National Highlights Inc.
Editor: Andrew Luke
Interior and cover design: Jana Rade, impact studios
Production: Michelle Luke

QR CODES AND LINKS TO THIRD-PARTY CONTENT

CONTENTS

KEY ICONS TO LOOK FOR:

 Words to Understand: These words with their easy-to-understand definitions will increase the reader's understanding of the text while building vocabulary skills.

 Sidebars: This boxed material within the main text allows readers to build knowledge, gain insights, explore possibilities, and broaden their perspectives by weaving together additional information to provide realistic and holistic perspectives.

 Educational Videos: Readers can view videos by scanning our QR codes, providing them with additional educational content to supplement the text. Examples include news coverage, moments in history, speeches, iconic sports moments and much more!

 Text-Dependent Questions: These questions send the reader back to the text for more careful attention to the evidence presented there.

 Research Projects: Readers are pointed toward areas of further inquiry connected to each chapter. Suggestions are provided for projects that encourage deeper research and analysis.

 Series Glossary of Key Terms: This back-of-the book glossary contains terminology used throughout this series. Words found here increase the reader's ability to read and comprehend higher-level books and articles in this field.

WORDS TO UNDERSTAND

PASSER RATING – a quarterback performance measurement used in NFL football

PLUMMETED – dropped or fell sharply and abruptly

PROLIfiC – marked by abundant inventiveness or productivity

CHAPTER 1

GREATEST MOMENTS

AARON RODGERS' NFL CAREER

There was some interest and expectations surrounding Aaron Rodgers coming out of college. The young quarterback (QB) from Chico, CA, was born December 2, 1983. Rodgers was drafted by the Green Bay Packers with the 24th pick in the 2005 NFL Draft. Rodgers was projected to go as high as the number one overall pick to his favorite childhood team, the San Francisco 49ers. The 49ers, instead, chose QB Alex Smith out of the University of Utah with the number one pick, and Rodgers' position in the first round of the draft plummeted.

What was thought of as a curious draft pick by Green Bay, given that the team already had Hall of Fame quarterback Brett Favre, turned out to be a great selection for the team and an investment in the team's future. Since he took over as the Packers quarterback in 2008, Rodgers has posted a 94–47 win-loss record, completed 65.2% of his passes, and thrown for 38,212 yards and 310 touchdowns against 75 interceptions.

He is the first QB in NFL history to throw 300 TDs before throwing 100 interceptions.

AARON RODGERS VERSUS BRETT FAVRE

Aaron Rodgers sat on the Green Bay bench for three seasons learning the game behind arguably one of the greatest players ever to play the quarterback position, Brett Favre. Favre played much of his career with the Packers, leading them to a Super Bowl victory in 1997. Favre retired at or near the top of the following statistical categories for quarterbacks in the NFL all-time:

- 6,300 career passes completed (ranked first all-time)
- 10,169 career passes attempted (ranked first all-time)
- 71,838 career passing yards (ranked second all-time)
- 508 career passing touchdowns (ranked second all-time)

How do Aaron Rodgers' stats stack up against his former teammate and mentor? These are Rodgers' numbers to-date:

- 3,188 career passes completed (ranked twenty-first all-time); Favre completed 2,997 passes through his first nine full seasons.
- 4,895 career passes attempted (ranked twenty-ninth all-time); Favre attempted 4,927 passes through his first nine full seasons. (ranked thirty-first all-time)
- 38,502 career passing yards (ranked twentieth all-time); Favre threw for 34,706 yards through his first nine full seasons.
- 313 career passing touchdowns (ranked tenth all-time); Favre threw 255 touchdowns through his first nine full seasons.

Rodgers has the potential to eclipse Favre's numbers and establish himself as an equal in Packers lore, out of the shadow of Favre.

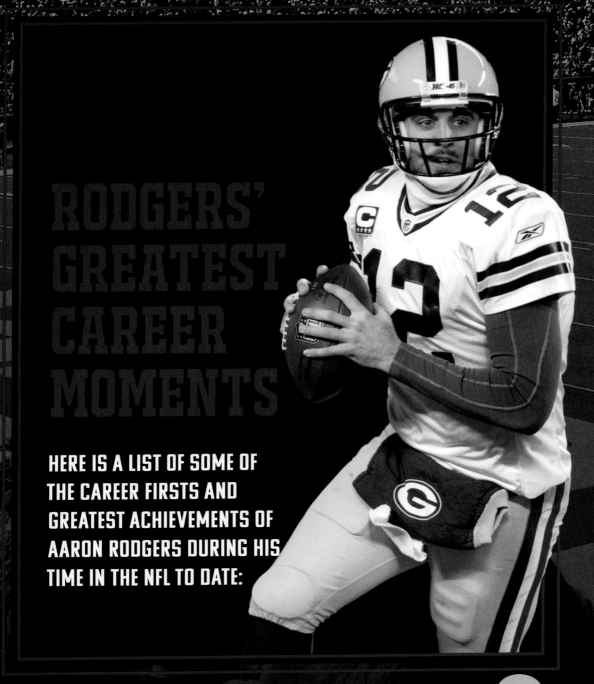

RODGERS' GREATEST CAREER MOMENTS

HERE IS A LIST OF SOME OF THE CAREER FIRSTS AND GREATEST ACHIEVEMENTS OF AARON RODGERS DURING HIS TIME IN THE NFL TO DATE:

FIRST CAREER TOUCHDOWN PASS

n what would be the last time Aaron Rodgers would perform mop-up duties for H
Famer Brett Favre (before assuming the reins of starting quarterback in the 2008 sea
Rodgers took advantage of an injury sustained by Favre to lead the Packers on a first-qu
drive deep into the Dallas Cowboys' red zone. With seconds left in the quarter, Rodge
wide receiver Greg Jennings on a crossing route, resulting in an 11-yard touchdown

An exuberant Rodgers
ran off the field,
clutching the football
that would represent
the first of his top-ten
career all-time total
n touchdown passes.

Aaron Rodgers, in the sixth game he participated in as a pro, throws an 11-yard touchdown pass to WR Greg Jennings in relief duty for an injured Brett Favre on November 29, 2007, against the Dallas Cowboys.

FIRST CAREER WIN

At the beginning of 2008 NFL season, Rodgers began his tenure at the helm of the offense as the starting quarterback for the Green Bay Packers. The Packers met division rival Minnesota to begin the 2008 season in a Monday night matchup at Lambeau Field in Green Bay. In the second half, Rodgers led the Packers on a 5-play, 62-yard drive that resulted in his first career touchdown pass as a starter in the NFL. The Packers went on to beat the Vikings 24–19.

Rodgers completed 81% of his passes in his first start, throwing the ball for 178 yards with no interceptions. Always mobile and athletic for a QB, he also rushed for 44 yards in his first career win.

Watch as Rodgers tosses one touchdown pass and runs for another as the starting QB of the Green Bay Packers, versus Minnesota Vikings, September 8, 2008.

FIRST 300-YARD PASSING GAME

The newly installed starting quarterback of the Green Bay Packers, on the heels of future Hall of Famer Brett Favre, followed up his first career victory as a starter by notching his second career win and passing the ball for 328 yards in his first career 300-yard passing game. Rodgers also completed his first multiple touchdown game, tossing three touchdowns in the winning effort against another division rival, the Detroit Lions. Rodgers went 24–38 (completions to attempts) for a completion percentage of 63% with no interceptions and a **passer rating** of 117.0.

Highlights of Aaron Rodgers passing for 300 yards for the first time in his career against the Detroit Lions, September 14, 2008 (Packers won the game 48–25).

FIRST 3,000+-YARD SEASON

The 2008 season proved to be a special one for Aaron Rodgers. Although the team finished with a 6–10 record, he finished the season by establishing himself as the "leader of the Pack." His 4,038 yards passing on 341 completions in 536 attempts, 28 touchdowns, and rating of 93.2 was the first time he surpassed 3,000 yards passing in a season. Since becoming the starting quarterback for the Packers, Rodgers has thrown for at least 2,500 or more yards in nine of the ten seasons from 2008—2017. He threw for more than 4,000 yards in six of those ten seasons (with no signs of slowing down).

Highlights of Aaron Rodgers first season as the starting quarterback for the Green Bay Packers in 2008, where he passed for 4,038 yards, 28 touchdowns, and 13 interceptions.

FIRST PLAYOFF VICTORY

Aaron Rodgers' first career playoff victory came in a wild card matchup against the Philadelphia Eagles on January 9, 2011. After closing out the 2010 season with wins against the New York Giants and Chicago Bears to earn a playoff berth, the Packers faced a 10–6 Eagles team on the road at Lincoln Financial Field in Philadelphia. Green Bay struck first, taking a 7–0 first quarter lead on a 7-yard touchdown pass to TE Tom Crabtree. Rodgers also tossed touchdown scores to WR James Jones and RB Brandon Jackson for a 21–16 win. Rodgers would go on to lead the team to two more road playoff wins en route to an appearance in Super Bowl XLV.

Check out Aaron Rodgers' 16-yard screen pass to running back Brandon James for a third quarter touchdown in a wild card playoff game against the Philadelphia Eagles, January 9, 2011.

FIRST SUPER BOWL VICTORY

Aaron Rodgers' 2010 season was as magical as one could be for any NFL player. The Rodgers-led Packers won the last two games of their season to grab the final NFC playoff spot. Playing on the road, the team won against Philadelphia in a wild card matchup (21–16); Atlanta in the divisional game (48–21); and division rival Chicago Bears in the NFC Championship game (21–14). Playing in Super Bowl XLV on February 6, 2011, Rodgers completed 61.5% of his passes for 3 touchdowns, 304 yards, and a passer rating of 111.5 as the Green Bay Packers defeated the Pittsburgh Steelers 31–25. He was named MVP of Super Bowl XLV.

Watch these video highlights from NFL.com of Aaron Rodgers and the Green Bay Packers' victory over the Pittsburgh Steelers in Super Bowl XLV, February 6, 2011.

REACHING THE 10,000-PASSING-YARDS PLATEAU

Passing the football for 3,000 yards in a season is a benchmark every NFL quarterback looks to accomplish in his career. Reaching the 10,000-passing-yard mark is one that is even harder yet, given the possibility of injury and inconsistent play that could quickly end a promising career. Aaron Rodgers is one of only 186 QBs to surpass 10,000 yards in passing, having done so in a game against Washington on October 10, 2010, only three seasons since taking the helm of the team as its passing leader.

This highlight shows Aaron Rodgers connecting with wide receiver James Jones on a 35-yard 1st-quarter catch on his way to reaching the 10,000-yard career passing mark in a game against Washington, October 10, 2010.

ore, either to tie or win a game, as time is expiring on the game clock. No quarterback has onstrated a more **prolific** gift for throwing and successfully completing this pass than n Rodgers. In a thirteen-month span beginning in the 2015 season, Rodgers threw 3(!) ssful Hail Mary's. The most famous of these was dubbed The Miracle in Motown, taking in Week 13 of the 2015 season in Detroit against the Lions. It was December 3, 2015, and

Bay trailed Detroit
.. With 0:00 on the
, Rodgers threw a
rd bomb for a TD
hard Rodgers (no
on) for the win.

A compilation of Aaron Rodgers throwing three Hail Mary passes in games against the Detroit Lions, Arizona Cardinals, and the New York Giants.

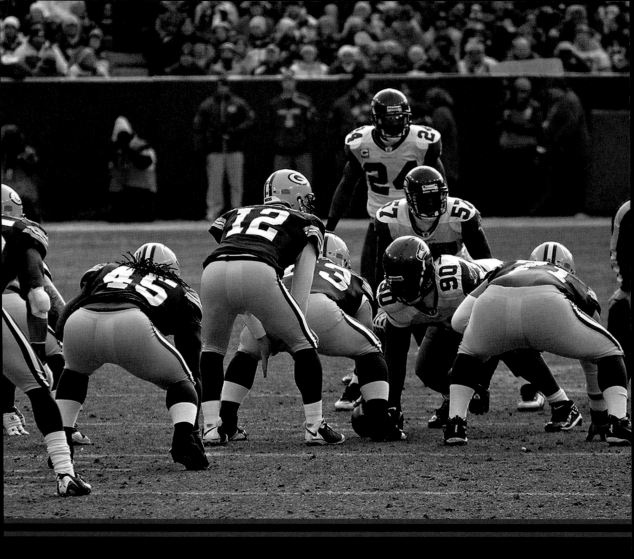

TEXT-DEPENDENT QUESTIONS:

1. What was Aaron Rodgers' projected draft position in the 2005 NFL Draft? Which player was selected first overall in that draft?

2. How many seasons as the starting quarterback for the Green Bay Packers did it take for Rodgers to surpass 10,000 career passing yards?

3. How many times has Rodgers passed for 2,500 yards in a season?

Aaron Rodgers is one of fourty-four quarterbacks in the history of the NFL to pass for more than 30,000 yards in their career. He has averaged, in just ten seasons (thirteen overall) as the starting quarterback for the Packers, 2,961 yards passing per season. 3,000 yards passing in a season is the success benchmark used for NFL quarterbacks. The benchmark for running backs and wide receivers is 1,000 yards (rushing and receiving). Which do you think is more difficult to accomplish in a season, passing for 3,000 yards, rushing for 1,000 yards, or gaining 1,000 yards in receiving yards? Look up the NFL statistics for quarterbacks, running backs, and wide receivers from 2012–2016 (five years) and determine how many QBs, RBs, and WRs achieved the benchmark in each of the five seasons. Have the number of players in each of these categories increased, decreased, or stayed the same year-to-year? Show your results in a chart.

WORDS TO UNDERSTAND

FBS – the abbreviation for Football Bowl Subdivision, the top college football tier (formerly Division 1A)

STELLAR – outstanding, spectacular, or extraordinary

VARSITY – the highest level of competition at the interscholastic (high school) or intercollegiate (college) levels

CHAPTER 2

THE ROAD TO THE TOP

ATHLETIC ACCOMPLISHMENTS IN HIGH SCHOOL AND COLLEGE

Aaron Rodgers was born in Chico, CA, a town of about 88,000 residents located in the Sacramento Valley, roughly ninety miles to the north of the city of Sacramento (the state capital). The town is best known as the home of the Sierra Nevada Brewing Company, and Build.com, an online home improvement retailer. The town is also the home to Chico State University.

Aaron, the middle child of three siblings, including Luke (oldest) and Jordan (youngest), was raised in a sports-minded household. The Rodgers excelled at various sports, including baseball, basketball, and football, which the brothers played in high school. Aaron and Jordan played on through college and at the professional level. Youngest brother Jordan Rodgers played college football at Vanderbilt University, finishing his career at the SEC school as 7th all-time in career offensive production. He

Early video from Aaron Rodgers's playing days at Pleasant Valley High School in Chico, CA. As you watch #12 play, you can see the pro-style form, arm strength, and presence that would carry him from high-school glory to become a two-time NFL MVP and Super Bowl Champion.

spent time in the camps and on the practice squads of the Jacksonville Jaguars, Tampa Bay Buccaneers, and Miami Dolphins of the NFL, as well as with the British Columbia Lions of the Canadian Football League before leaving professional football in 2015.

HIGH SCHOOL

Aaron Rodgers played quarterback for two years at Chico's Pleasant Valley High School. As a member of the Viking's football squad, Rodgers led the team in 2000–2001 to an overall

17–7 record. He also led the Vikings to consecutive first-round playoff appearances in the California Interscholastic Federation's North Section. He posted back-to-back 2,000-yard passing seasons, throwing for 2,103 yards in his junior year and 2,318 yards as a senior.

In addition to starring on the football team, Rodgers played **varsity** basketball for Pleasant Valley. He was on the basketball team for three years and played baseball and soccer as well. On the subject of playing more than one sport in high school, Rodgers recounted in a January 2017 interview posted on the Philadelphia Inquirer newspaper's website:

"It definitely helped me because I learned different skills in different sports, and there are competitive things that run through all the sports. I was always drawn to being in positions where I had an impact on the game: point guard in basketball, pitcher in baseball, goalie or forward in soccer. I wanted to be in those premiere positions where you're having a direct impact on the game, and you learn a lot of skills along the way to take advantage of little nuances in the game. It helps.

"I think kids can get burnt out playing AAU basketball the entire year or traveling baseball the entire year. Football, we don't really have a ton of that, with the entire-year stuff. But I think it's going to be important for kids to not be as one-sport-centered as we move forward. ... You want to see guys who are playing multiple sports and have that competitiveness because a well-rounded athlete, I think, is going to be better with adversity."

COLLEGE

Although he posted impressive stats as a high-school quarterback, he did not receive much attention from college recruiters. The top recruits in 2000–2001 coming out of high school who were highly recruited over Rodgers include Brock Berlin from Shreveport,

LA, a Parade All-American and Gatorade National Player of the Year who played briefly in the NFL with Miami, Dallas, St. Louis Rams, and Detroit Lions; Jason Campbell of Taylorsville, MS, who after a stellar career at Auburn was drafted as the 25th pick in the 2005 draft by Washington; and John Brodie Coyle from Rainbow City, AL, and the University of Alabama. Coyle was a third-round selection of the Kansas City Chiefs in 2006 who after five seasons with the Chiefs, spent a brief two years on the practice squad of the Arizona Cardinals.

As Rodgers was not recruited by any of the top FBS schools, he chose to attend Butte College, a community college located in Oroville, CA. While at Butte, he led the Roadrunners to a 10–1 record in his first year and a NorCal Conference championship. His 30 touchdowns earned him third-team junior college All-American honors and the attention of University of California Golden Bears Head Coach Jeff Tedford (now head

After a year at junior college, Rodgers transferred to the University of California at Berkeley to start at QB for the Golden Bears.

Rodgers skipped his senior season
at Cal to enter the 2005 NFL Draft.

coach for the Fresno University Bulldogs). Rodgers transferred in 2003 to California to begin play in the Pac-10 conference.

As a FBS-level player, Rodgers outshined the competition. Rodgers led the Golden Bears to a 7–3 overall record in his inaugural season. He completed 61.6% of his passes (215 completions in 349 passing attempts) for 2,903 yards and 19 touchdowns. He also gained 210 yards rushing and recorded 5 touchdowns. His efforts helped California gain an invite to the 2003 Insight Bowl against the Virginia Tech Hokies. The game ended in a 52–49 win for California. Rodgers's 394-yard, 2-touchdown passing, and 2-touchdown rushing performance earned him MVP honors for the game.

Rodgers returned to California for his junior year. The 2004 season saw the Golden Bears finish the season at 10–1, with their only loss coming to USC, 23–17. Rodgers

Quarterback Alex Smith was drafted first overall in 2005 by the San Francisco 49ers.

finished the season passing for 2,506 yards, tossing 24 touchdowns and completing 66.1% of his passes, while rushing for 3 touchdowns. The team would face the Texas Tech Raiders in the Holiday Bowl on December 30, 2004. The Golden Bears lost in this matchup, 45–31, with Rodgers passing for 246 yards, completing 57.1% of his passes, throwing 1 touchdown, and rushing for 1 touchdown.

NFL DRAFT DAY 2005

After the bowl loss to the Raiders in 2004, Rodgers decided to forego his final year of NCAA eligibility and enter the 2005 NFL Draft. Rodgers participated in the 2005 NFL Scouting Combine, where he posted the following results:

- Measurements (height, weight): 6' 2" (1.88 m), 223 lbs (101 kg)
- 40-yard dash: 4.71 seconds

- 3-cone: 7.39 seconds
- Vertical jump: 34.5 inches (0.88 m)
- Broad jump: 9' 2" 9 (2.79 m)

No other quarterback taken in his draft class has had anywhere near Rodgers' success. He has well over 100 more touchdowns than the next closest player.

On the famous Wonderlic test, used to assess a player's intelligence, Rodgers scored a 35/50, which is considered an exceptional score and well over the average score of 24 for quarterbacks.

Rodgers very much expected to be selected high in the NFL draft and wanted to play for his favorite team, the San Francisco 49ers, who controlled the number one overall pick. As draft day came closer, many scouts doubted Rodgers's abilities and questioned whether he was ready to step in as a starter in the NFL. Because of these doubts, Aaron Rodgers's stock fell from that of a potential number one pick to a project with upside, and it was at the number 24 pick where the Green Bay Packers chose him as a potential heir to Brett Favre's throne.

Aaron Rodgers's fall from potential number one to 24 is considered one of the top ten NFL draft moments, according to NFL Network. The San Francisco 49ers, for

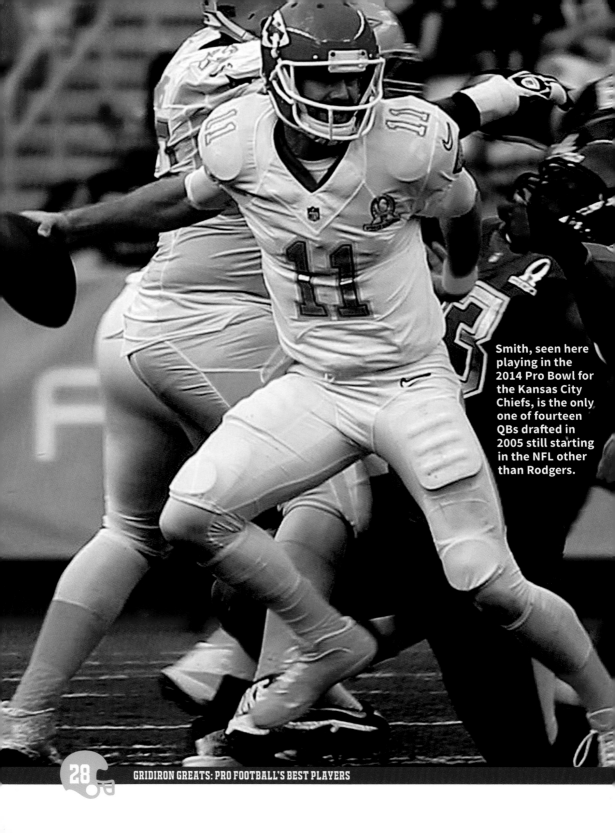

Smith, seen here playing in the 2014 Pro Bowl for the Kansas City Chiefs, is the only one of fourteen QBs drafted in 2005 still starting in the NFL other than Rodgers.

their part, drafted University of Utah quarterback Alex Smith with the number one pick as a replacement for Tim Rattay (currently the quarterbacks coach at Louisiana Tech University).

It is said that the NFL draft is as much art as it is science. Picking a potential superstar and future Hall of Fame player requires more than an analysis of statistics; it also requires a sense and feel for how the player will fit into the team's system. The 49ers' selection of Smith was thought to fulfill an immediate need they had for a pro-style quarterback. Rodgers was the second quarterback chosen in the 2005 draft, followed immediately by Jason Campbell from Auburn University to Washington with the 25th pick, the draft's third selection at the quarterback position.

RESEARCH PROJECT

A quarterback gene runs in the Rodgers family. Aaron's younger brother Jordan also followed his played QB, spending time with Jacksonville, Miami, and Tampa Bay, as well as a brief stint with the British Columbia Lions of the Canadian Football League before retiring from the game in 2015. Find and list the pairs of brothers who played the game at the NFL level over the past fifty years (1967–2016).

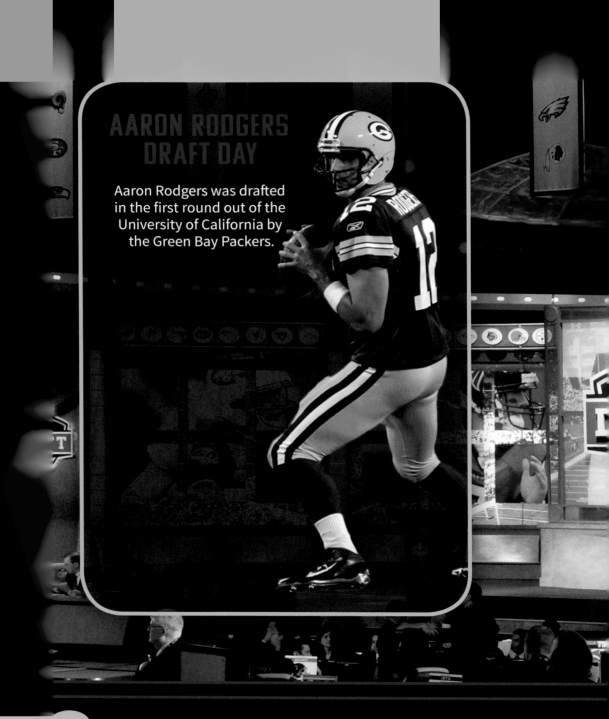

AARON RODGERS DRAFT DAY

Aaron Rodgers was drafted in the first round out of the University of California by the Green Bay Packers.

NFL DRAFT DAY 2005
SIGNIFICANT ACCOUNTS

- The 2005 NFL draft was held at the Jacob K. Javits Convention Center located in New York City. It was the first time the draft was not held in Madison Square Garden since 1995.

- Aaron Rodgers was the 24th overall selection in the draft. Alex Smith, the overall number one draft selection, was picked by the San Francisco 49ers, Rodgers's favorite team.

- Rodgers was the second quarterback drafted in the 2005 NFL Draft.

- Aaron Rodgers was one of fourteen quarterbacks taken in the 2005 NFL Draft.

- Of the fourteen quarterbacks selected, only six are still active in the NFL (2017) and two are starters (Smith for the Kansas City Chiefs and Rodgers for the Green Bay Packers).

- Linebacker was the most commonly selected position, with thirty-six taken. The first linebacker selected was DeMarcus Ware of Troy, who went 11th to Dallas.

- Three of the top five players selected played the running back position, beginning with second pick Ronnie Brown of Auburn, who was taken by Miami.

- The Tampa Bay Buccaneers had the most selections in the draft, with twelve. Tampa Bay's first selection was another Auburn running back, Carnell "Cadillac" Williams, at 5th overall.

- The New York Giants had the fewest selections in the draft, with just four in seven rounds.

RODGERS VERSUS 2005 NFL QUARTERBACK DRAFT CLASS

How do the careers of Rodgers, who has only been a member of the Green Bay Packers, and Alex Smith (who played seven seasons with San Francisco before heading east to play with the Kansas City Chiefs) compare?

Player	NFL Team(s)	Yards	Comp%	TDs	Rating
Aaron Rodgers	Packers	38,502	65.1	313	103.8
Alex Smith	49ers/Chiefs	31,888	62.4	183	94.8

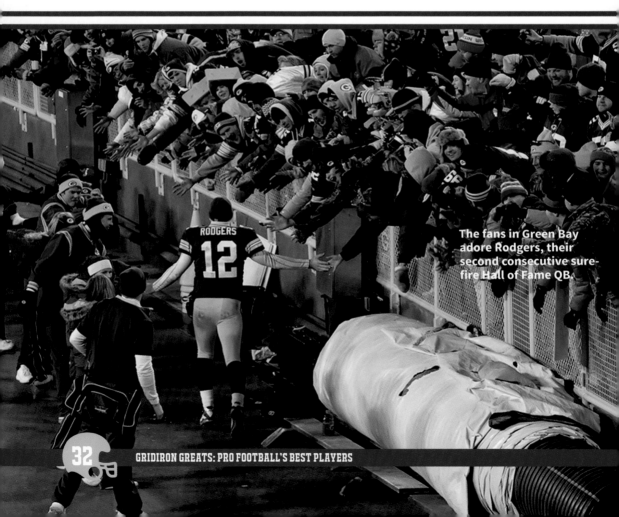

The fans in Green Bay adore Rodgers, their second consecutive sure-fire Hall of Fame QB.

Rodgers has been the leader of the Packers for more than a decade.

Smith has been a starter at the quarterback position for twelve NFL seasons beginning in week five of the 2005 season (the 2008 season was lost to injury), while Rodgers has completed ten full seasons in the position through 2017. No one would have predicted that after thirteen seasons in the NFL, Aaron Rodgers would be the better of the two quarterbacks coming out of the 2005 draft.

There was a total of fourteen quarterbacks selected in the draft. Six of the fourteen drafted in 2005 are still playing in the league today (including Dan Orlovsky, who is a free agent that played the 2017 preseason for the Los Angeles Rams) and only two started for their respective teams as of the end of the 2017 NFL season (Rodgers for the Packers, Smith for the Chiefs).

Here are the important statistics for each of the quarterbacks drafted in 2005:

Player (School)	Round/Pick	NFL Team	Yards	TDs	Rating	Pro-Bowl(s)	MVP(s)
Aaron Rodgers (California)	1/24	Green Bay	38,502	313	103.8	6	2
Alex Smith (Utah)	1/1	San Francisco	27,846	183	94.8	2	0
Ryan Fitzpatrick (Harvard)	7/250	St. Louis	26,991	173	79.9	0	0
Kyle Orton (Purdue)	4/106	Chicago	18,037	101	81.2	0	0
Matt Cassel (USC)	7/230	New England	17,449	104	78.8	1	0
Jason Campbell (Auburn)	1/25	Washington	16,771	87	81.7	0	0
Derek Anderson (Oregon State)	6/213	Baltimore	10,413	60	71.1	1	0
Charlie Frye (Akron)	3/65	Cleveland	4,154	17	69.7	0	0
Dan Orlovsky (Connecticut)	5/145	Detroit	3,132	15	75.3	0	0
Andrew Walter (Arizona State)	3/69	Oakland	1,919	3	52.6	0	0
David Greene (Georgia)	3/85	Seattle	0	0	0	0	0
Stefan LeFors (Louisville)	4/121	Carolina	0	0	0	0	0
Adrian McPherson (Florida State)	5/152	New Orleans	0	0	0	0	0
James Kilian (Tulsa)	7/229	Kansas City	0	0	0	0	0

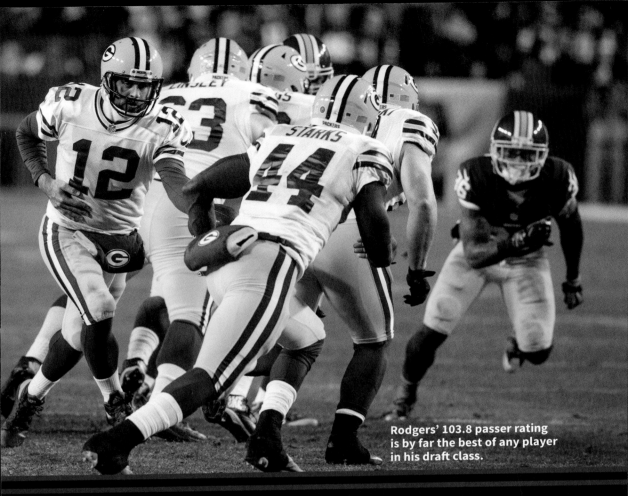

Rodgers' 103.8 passer rating is by far the best of any player in his draft class.

TEXT-DEPENDENT QUESTIONS:

1. How many quarterbacks were drafted in the 2005 NFL Draft? How many of those quarterbacks are still in the NFL as of 2017? Which of those players drafted start at the quarterback position?

2. How many NFL teams has Aaron Rodgers played for in his career? How many NFL teams has Alex Smith played for in his career?

3. How many points above the average for NFL quarterbacks did Aaron Rodgers score on the Wonderlic test administered prior to the NFL draft?

WORDS TO UNDERSTAND

APT – being to the point

ENSHRINED – to remember and protect (someone or something that is valuable, admired, etc)

EXTRAPOLATE – to predict by projecting past experience or known data

LAUD – to praise (someone or something)

PREDECESSOR – a person who held a job or position before someone else

CHAPTER 3

ON THE FIELD

CAREER COMPARISONS

There are a lot of arguments to be made for placing Aaron Rodgers on the list of greatest NFL quarterbacks. Contemporaries such as Tom Brady, Peyton Manning, and Brett Favre certainly stand in a class of their own, but it is difficult not to laud Rodgers and his accomplishments to-date.

It can be argued that even if Rodgers is not quite at the Brady/Manning/Favre level yet, he is certainly in the class of QBs such as Joe Montana, Fran Tarkenton, John Elway, and Johnny Unitas, all of whom are members of Pro Football's Hall of Fame. It can be further argued that Rodgers, in nine full seasons, has already exceeded the careers of Jim Kelly and Troy Aikman.

The comparisons between Aaron Rodgers and Brett Favre seem a bit too obvious because of the fact that Rodgers took over the team after Favre retired in 2008. A comparison with Tom Brady, a quarterback with a similar style to that of Rodgers', would seem more appropriate, given that both players are still in the league and considered the top two QBs in the league (depending on who is ranking them).

Here is a comparison of the two players' careers through the end of the 2017 season:

Player	W–L(W%)	CMP%	YDS	TD	INT
Aaron Rodgers	94-48 (.662)	65.1%	38,502	313	78
Tom Brady	196-55 (.781)	63.9%	66,159	488	160

Since Aaron Rodgers did not start at the quarterback position until his fourth season in the league (for Brady it was in his second professional season), a more apt comparison would be that of each quarterback's first nine seasons:

Player	W–L(W%)	CMP%	YDS	TD	INT
Aaron Rodgers	90–45 (.667)	65.2%	36,498	296	71
Tom Brady	97–30 (.764)	63.4%	30,838	225	99

When comparing the early career records of these two great quarterbacks destined to be enshrined in the Hall of Fame, it is not difficult to see that Rodgers was as successful if not a better quarterback than Tom Brady. This is a high standard to measure against, as many experts consider Brady to be the best QB of all time.

If Rodgers is lucky enough to match Brady's health and longevity (Rodgers's 2017 season ended after six games due to injury), given his career to-date and what his average production has been as a quarterback for the nine seasons he has started, we can extrapolate the data to show that he has a chance to statistically be the greatest quarterback ever in the game:

Over his first nine seasons as a starter, Rodgers' stats compare favorably to those of Tom Brady, considered by many to be the best QB ever to play.

	W–L	CMP%	YDS	TD	INT
8 more seasons:	170–85	65.2%	69,267	561	136
10 more seasons:	186–95	65.2%	77,377	627	152

This assumes, of course, that he maintains the same level of production as he ages. Rodgers would be 41 in 2024. 77,000 career passing yards would, however, almost certainly be the most of all time. Current career passing yards leader Peyton Manning has fewer than 72,000. Manning also leads with 539 career touchdowns—a mark Rodgers could break before age 40.

AARON RODGERS
GREEN BAY PACKERS

QUARTERBACK

AARON RODGERS

Date of birth: December 2, 1983;
Height: 6 feet 2 inches (1.88 m), **Weight:** 223 lbs (101 kg);
Drafted in the first round in 2005 (24th pick overall) by the Green Bay Packers
College: University of California, Berkeley

CAREER

GAMES	COMPLETIONS	ATTEMPTS	COMP%	YARDS	TDS	INT
149	3188	4895	65.1	38,502	313	78

- Was named NFL league MVP twice—2011 and 2014
- Named to six Pro Bowls
- Made first-team NFL All-Pro twice in his career—2011 and 2014
- Led Packers to Super Bowl XLV victory over the Pittsburgh Steelers, 31–25, February 6, 2011
- 104.1 quarterback rating (first all-time for NFL career)
- Only NFL quarterback in the history of the NFL with a career rating over 100
- Best TD-to-INT ratio in NFL history (4.13)
- Holds NFL record for most TD passes in a half (6—November 9, 2014, vs. Chicago)
- Holds NFL record for most passes of more than 70 yards (16)
- Was the Offensive MVP, Insight Bowl (2003)
- Received First-Team All-Pac 10 honors (2004)
- Played high school football, basketball, baseball, and soccer at Pleasant Valley High School (Chico, CA)–Nickname: Vikings

QUARTERBACK

It took Aaron Rodgers just three seasons as a starter to pass for more than 10,000 yards in his career. Rodgers continues to rack up the yards, surpassing 20,000 yards in a December 2, 2012, game against the Minnesota Vikings, and reaching 30,000 yards after eight full seasons against San Diego in 2015. With more than 38,000 career yards under his belt, Rodgers is on his way to reaching 40,000 during the 2018 season, something only eighteen other quarterbacks have accomplished in the history of the NFL.

Watch Aaron Rodgers complete a touchdown pass to WR Randall Cobb to end the 2016 season with 4,428 yards passing against the Detroit Lions, January 1, 2017.

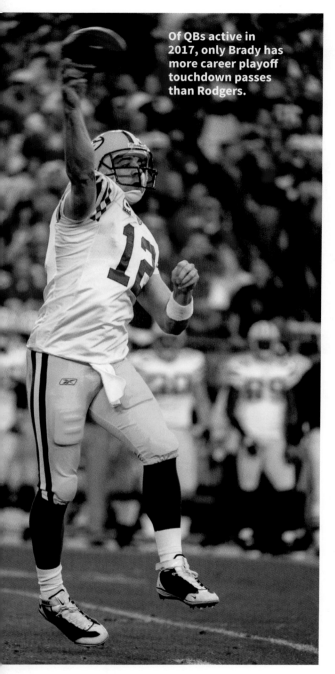

Of QBs active in 2017, only Brady has more career playoff touchdown passes than Rodgers.

AARON RODGERS IN THE PLAYOFFS

Since becoming the Packer's starting quarterback, Aaron Rodgers has made sixteen appearances in the playoffs. This includes six wild card games, posting a win-loss record of 4–2 (.667 winning percentage), six divisional playoff games (3–3 record for a .500 winning percentage), three NFC championship games (1–2, .333 winning percentage), and one Super Bowl appearance (XLV), which he won in 2011.

Over his playoff career to-date, his quarterback rating is 99.4, which is just below two Hall of Fame quarterbacks Bart Starr (a former Green Bay Packer player and head coach) and Kurt Warner, as well as current players Matt Ryan (Atlanta Falcons) and Drew Brees (New Orleans Saints).

Career Playoff Quarterback Rating

Rank	Player	RAT	Team(s)	Years
1	Bart Starr+	104.8	Green Bay Packers	(1956–1971)
2	Kurt Warner+	102.8	St Louis Rams/Arizona Cardinals	(1998–2009)
3	Matt Ryan	100.8	Atlanta Falcons	(2008–present)
4	Drew Brees	100.7	SD Chargers/New Orleans Saints	(2001–present)
5	Aaron Rodgers	99.4	Green Bay Packers	(2005–present)

+Enshrined in the NFL Hall of Fame

Comparing Rodgers and his playoff stats to that of current active players in the league shows that he is among the elite quarterbacks, second only to Tom Brady of the New England Patriots in terms of experience and results:

Player	W–L	CMP%	YDS	TD	INT	RAT
Matt Ryan	4–6 (.400)	67.5%	2672	20	7	100.8
Drew Brees	7–6 (.538)	65.9%	4209	29	9	100.7
Aaron Rodgers	9–7 (.563)	63.5%	4458	36	10	99.4
Russell Wilson	8–4 (.667)	61.6%	2777	20	11	94.1
Tom Brady	28–9 (.757)	63.0%	9721	68	31	90.1
Joe Flacco	10–5 (.667)	56.6%	3223	25	10	88.6
Eli Manning	8–4 (.667)	60.5%	2815	18	9	87.4
Ben Roethlisberger	13–8 (.619)	62.4%	5256	30	24	86.5
Phillip Rivers	4–5 (.444)	60.3%	2165	11	9	85.2
Andrew Luck	3–3 (.500)	56.5%	1829	9	12	70.8

MULTI-SPORT ADVANTAGE

Aaron Rodgers credits much of his durability and longevity in the league (thirteen years in the NFL, ten years as a starting quarterback as of the end of the 2017 season) to having played multiple sports while in high school in Chico, CA. The conditioning and skill sets that he learned playing baseball, basketball, and soccer has helped his footwork, awareness, and allowed him to play in 142 of the 160 games he has been designated to start (a 90% playing/participation rate).

Green Bay Packers QB Aaron Rodgers, prior to the start of the 2011 season, shows fine form delivering a perfect strike before the start of a Milwaukee Brewers baseball game.

Aaron Rodgers is one of the few players in NFL history to win the league's MVP award multiple times. Rodgers was named MVP in 2011 and again in 2014. His predecessor Bret Favre was also a multiple league MVP, having been so named three times in his career (1995, 1996, 1997). How many players in the history of the league, beginning in 1957, received MVP honors multiple times? Research this information through books and online sources and generate a list including the player's name, team, position, and years the award was received.

Rodgers's playoff statistics are not only good as compared with current quarterbacks in the game, his numbers also compare more than favorably to some of the all-time greatest quarterbacks to play, such as his **predecessor** Brett Favre, Peyton Manning, John Elway, and Dan Marino, among others:

Player	W-L	CMP%	YDS	TD	INT	RAT
Aaron Rodgers	9–7 (.563)	63.5%	4458	36	10	99.4
Joe Montana+	16–7 (.696)	62.7%	5772	45	21	95.6
Troy Aikman+	11–4 (.733)	63.7%	3849	23	17	88.3
Peyton Manning	14–13 (.519)	63.2%	7339	40	25	87.4
Brett Favre+	13–11 (.542)	60.8%	5855	44	30	86.3
Steve Young+	8–6 (.571)	62.0%	3326	20	13	85.8
Terry Bradshaw+	14–5 (.737)	57.2%	3833	30	26	83.0
John Elway+	14–7 (.667)	54.5%	4964	27	21	79.7
Dan Marino+	8–10 (.444)	56.0%	4510	32	24	77.1
Jim Kelly+	9–8 (.529)	59.1%	3863	21	28	72.3

+Enshrined in the NFL Hall of Fame

Imagine the type of career numbers in both the regular season and playoffs Aaron Rodgers would have had if he had started playing quarterback in the 2005 season. Regardless, it is clear that the type of career that he has had to-date in the NFL is more than the majority of NFL players can dream of and is certainly better than that of the thirteen other quarterbacks taken in the same NFL Draft. We may only just be at the beginning of the second half of the career of Rodgers, so there is still plenty more of his greatness to come, as he is showing no signs of slowing down anytime soon.

Rodgers' career on the field to-date puts him on a trajectory toward the Pro Football Hall of Fame.

TEXT-DEPENDENT QUESTIONS:

1. What is Aaron Rodgers's career passer rating during the regular season? What is his career passing rating in the playoffs?
2. How many times was Rodgers named to the Pro Bowl? How many times was he named to the NFL All-Pro team?
3. For which college bowl was Rodgers named offensive MVP in 2003?

WORDS TO UNDERSTAND

AUDIBLE – heard or capable of being heard

LACKLUSTER – lacking liveliness, vitality, spirit, or enthusiasm

MEME – a cultural item in the form of an image, video, phrase, etc , that is spread via the Internet and often altered in a creative or humorous way

CHAPTER 4

WORDS COUNT

When the time comes to address the media pre- or post-game, players either retreat to the comfort of the safe position that avoids controversy (Cliché City), or they speak their mind with refreshing candor (Quote Machine).

Here are ten quotes from Aaron Rodgers, compiled in part from the website 247Sports. com, with some insight as to the context of what he is talking about or referencing:

Rodgers can be very outspoken when discussing the prospects of his team.

"**Playing behind a first-ballot Hall of Famer, who also is the all-time record holder for consecutive starts by a quarterback, it's a different mind-set. You just have to challenge yourself in ways that you never challenged yourself before.**"

Aaron Rodgers entered the 2005 NFL Draft, foregoing his senior year at California, because he believed he would be drafted in the top five. However, some negative opinions about his abilities and readiness to play at the pro level created an environment of doubt and fear among the twenty-one teams that did not draft Rodgers ahead of the Packers. Rodgers understood fully his position when he was picked by Green Bay; he was going to be looking at lot of bench time (about three seasons' worth) sitting behind one of the greatest quarterbacks the NFL has ever seen in Brett Favre. Rodgers prepared himself mentally and physically to be ready to step up when called upon. When Favre announced his retirement from the NFL at the end of the 2007 season, Rodgers put down his clipboard as the backup and has never looked back. **Rating: Quote Machine**

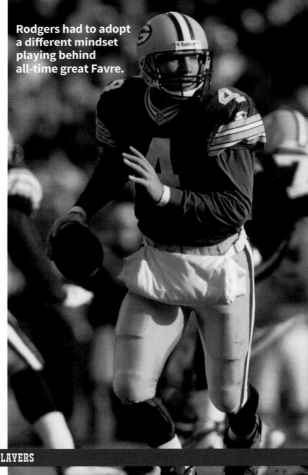

Rodgers had to adopt a different mindset playing behind all-time great Favre.

"Performing at my best is important to me and should be to everyone. I am blessed that my dad is a chiropractor. Getting adjusted regularly— along with practicing other good health habits that my mom helped me establish—are all part of my goal to win in life and on the field."

Rodgers credits a lot of his work ethic and the way in which he goes about preparing for the game to the lessons taught to him by his parents, Edward and Darla Rodgers. This particular quote, however, comes across like an ad for his father's services. **Rating: Cliché City**

This quote speaks to Rodgers' desire to become one of the best, if not the best quarterback in the history of the NFL. Sitting for three years behind Hall of Fame QB Brett Favre afforded Rodgers an apprenticeship most quarterbacks do not receive. This has translated to two MVP awards, two All-Pro selections and a Super Bowl ring. **Rating: Quote Machine**

"I know I'm capable of greatness, and I'm expecting to reach that level."

"The guys who stick around are the smartest guys and the guys who are the most self-driven. You have to have drive. The coaches can only take you so far. You have to want to learn and work."

Rodgers understands the importance of having good coaches; in his career, he has played for the same franchise (Green Bay Packers) and has started under the same head coach (Mike McCarthy) in each of his nine seasons. That consistency has allowed him to work through some early mechanical issues and develop into a superstar passer. He knows that the work that he has done with the coaching staff can only take him so far. His personal drive and work ethic will help keep him in the league for a long time, playing at the highest level. **Rating: Quote Machine**

Rodgers has played only for head coach Mike McCarthy (L) in his career as a starter.

> "If we can string together some wins this year, maybe I'll be a close second or third behind Bart Starr on their favorite quarterback list."

This is a tongue in cheek quote that Rodgers made at the end of an interview with a Wisconsin newspaper before the start of the 2008 NFL season. It speaks to his acknowledgment of the difficulty of stepping into the shoes of a player the caliber of Brett Favre, and playing for an organization with a storied history where fans are accustomed to champions like Favre and Starr. **Rating: Quote Machine**

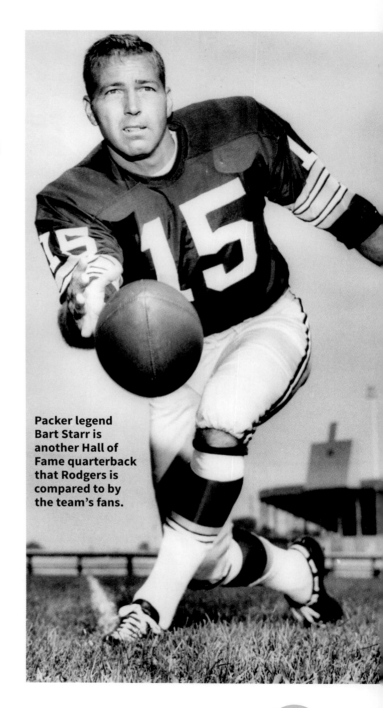

Packer legend Bart Starr is another Hall of Fame quarterback that Rodgers is compared to by the team's fans.

Rodgers has been relatively injury free throughout his career, although a broken collar bone limited him to just seven games in 2017

"**The thing you realize as you get older and you play, that you don't really understand when you're a backup the first few offseasons, is how important that mental rest is. It's a grind physically during the season, dealing with the hits and the physical pain that goes with playing in this game. But mentally it's probably more taxing, so you need that ability to find that escape.**"

Rodgers has been fortunate not to suffer many physical issues in his playing career, aside from a shoulder injury that kept him out for seven games in 2013, offseason surgery for a torn ACL before the start of the 2016 season, and a broken collarbone that ended his 2017 season at six games. Being physically fit to play football is tough, but being mentally fit to deal with the ups and downs of winning and losing, the pressure to perform, etc. is equally if not more important. **Rating: Quote Machine**

Aaron Rodgers learned from the best in Brett Favre on how to be a leader. This quote speaks to his approach to leading the team, and that his leadership on the field is more his personality than something that can be taught. **Rating: Quote Machine**

"**Leadership can't be forced or contrived. It has to be your personality.**"

"I've always been supremely confident in my abilities. But the biggest confidence boost is when the guys around you, you feel like they have confidence in you."

Aaron Rodgers relishes the role of leader, having been named a captain at California and for the Packers. His confidence not only comes from his belief in himself but also from the trust his teammates and the organization places in him, a cliché he reinforces with this quote. **Rating: Cliché City**

"Tonight is not a setback. It's just a learning experience."

Fans sometimes get frustrated with Rodgers's low-key reaction about losses. Staying low key and taking something from every experience has allowed him to continue to experience success at the NFL level. He has also learned when to speak his mind about losses and when to give the expected answer, as he did with this quote. **Rating: Cliché City**

"The challenge to be the best is what drives me and to just improve my body every day."

Another quote in which Rodgers discusses the importance of staying physically strong and active in order to stay on top of his game and play at the highest possible level, minus the effort to include any real insight. **Rating: Cliché City**

R-E-L-A-X

The start of Rodgers's and the Green Bay Packers' 2014 season was anything but relaxing. The team lost its opening game of the season before coming back to win in Week 2, only to drop a lackluster effort in Week 3 against division foe Detroit by the score of 19–7 on September 21, 2014.

During his weekly radio show on a local station in Milwaukee, WI, Rodgers was questioned about what appeared to be a lack of motivation as well as urgency to win. At this point in his career, Rodgers had been the starting quarterback for seven seasons, engineered a playoff appearance in the 2013 season when the team went 8–7–1 (while he was out on injury reserve for seven games), and had been named the league's most valuable player for the 2011 season (when the team posted a league best fifteen wins against one loss, fourteen of which are credited to Rodgers).

After listening to different theories as to why the team was not playing well (including some speculation that Rodgers's recent relationship with actress Olivia Munn was the cause of the team's start), he decided to set the record straight. When Rodgers began to speak, fielding the question as best as he could with the same calm and cool approach he takes when in a game situation, he provided this response to the nagging question of whether his team had the ability to compete and win this season:

"Five letters here, just for everybody out there in Packer-land and yourself today. R-E-L-A-X. We're going to be OK."

The words, which produced an audible laugh from the assembled fans and others, became an instant meme throughout the NFL. What were the results of Rodgers telling everyone to simply calm down? A four-game win streak followed closely by a five-game win streak, and then two closeout wins for a 12–4 overall record and a first-round playoff bye.

Rodgers famously told the Green Bay fans and media to "R-E-L-A-X" after a 1–2 start to the 2014 season.

There may be no more famous moment in Green Bay sports media than the time when Aaron Rodgers had to calm the fears of Packer fans and right the ship in 2014 on the way to the NFC Championship game. History repeated itself during the 2016 season when Packer fans were again nervous over the team's slow start. Rodgers pulled out his tried and tested R-E-L-A-X speech for fans after a November 20, 2016, loss to Washington. At 4–6, the team needed to run the table and win its remaining six games to have a chance at making the playoffs. The results? Six straight wins plus playoff victories over the NY Giants and Dallas Cowboys before losing in the NFC Championship game to Atlanta.

Aaron Rodgers speaking on ESPN's *First Take,* November 29, 2016, telling reporters that he had complete faith that the Packers can "run the table" to close out the 2016 season and recover from their 4-6 start.

That 2014 team was a botched-special-teams play away at the end of regulation in the NFC Championship game against Seattle from going to the Super Bowl. Rodgers won his second league MVP award that season.

AARON RODGERS ON COLIN KAEPERNICK AND RACIAL INJUSTICE IN THE NFL

An issue of note that has consumed the league is that of a person's free-speech rights and whether they extend to the football field (or to any sports field of competition) when the national anthem is played. One-time NFL QB Colin Kaepernick, the former signal caller for the San Francisco 49ers (who replaced

Rodgers believes that ex-QB Colin Kaepernick was excluded from the NFL in 2017 due to his high-profile stand on racial injustice.

RESEARCH PROJECT

Colin Kaepernick is not the first NFL player to use his status as a professional football player to bring light to an important issue. Do some research and find two additional instances where a player used their celebrity to bring attention to some issue affecting everyone. Define the issue and what it was the player did to effect change.

1. How many games did the Green Bay Packers lose before Aaron Rodgers announced that he would run the table to finish the 2016 NFL season?

2. Which of the great former Packer quarterbacks was Aaron Rodgers referring to when he spoke of how he needed to prepare himself to become a team leader?

3. How many NFL championships have the Green Bay Packers won? How many of those championships are Super Bowl Championships?

Alex Smith in that role) chose to kneel rather than stand during the singing of the national anthem before the start of a game during the 2016 season. The move is viewed by some as controversial and disrespectful, despite its motives to bring attention to issues of racial injustice and racial inequality in America. On the issue of Kaepernick's (or any player's) right to use the NFL as a platform to bring attention to issues, here is what Rodgers had to say:

"'I think [Kaepernick] should be on a roster right now,' Rodgers says in a wide-ranging interview with ESPN published on August 30, 2017. 'I think because of his protests, he's not.'

"'I think the best way I can say this is: I don't understand what it's like to be in that situation. What it is to be pulled over, or profiled, or any number of issues that have happened, that Colin was referencing—or any of my teammates have talked to me about . . . But I know it's a real thing my black teammates have to deal with.

"'I know he had a lot of fear about it, and how he would be accepted, and how people would change around him. I think society is finally moving in the right direction, as far as treating all people with respect and love and acceptance and appreciation. And in the locker room, I think the sport is getting closer."

WORDS TO UNDERSTAND

ACCOLADES – any award, honor, or laudatory notice

ESTRANGED – no longer friendly or close to another person or group

FODDER – experiences or material that is used to create interest or stir controversy

CHAPTER 5

OFF THE FIELD

A FAMILY AFFAIR: BROTHER VS. BROTHER

For as public as he is about his play on the field, the team's prospects and chances, and where he may rank in comparison with other quarterbacks in the league, both past and present, Aaron Rodgers is just as private when it comes to his personal life. Unlike other players in the NFL of his caliber talent wise, Rodgers tends to shy away from the spotlight and focus on improving his quarterback play. He is certainly one of the league's best players, and his play on the field speaks more than any words he chooses to say or activities that he involves himself with that are non-football related.

His brother Jordan is the former NFL and CFL quarterback who was recently hired by ESPN as an announcer for Southeastern Conference (SEC) games (Jordan Rodgers played quarterback for Vanderbilt University). Jordan appeared as a finalist on the 2016 edition of the television show *The Bachelorette*. Rodgers was chosen as the eventual winning suitor, and in a very public disclosure, mentioned how hurt he and members of his family, including their father Ed, were that Aaron was completely estranged from the family and not on speaking terms.

It had been rumored that the cause of the rift between Rodgers and his brothers and parents was actress Olivia Munn. Olivia Munn and Rodgers began a not-so-private relationship in 2014. The couple became an instant celebrity duo, as well as fodder for the entertainment tabloids. The public nature of the relationship was more than Rodgers was normally comfortable with but the relationship progressed. She moved to Green Bay to live with him during the 2015 and 2016 seasons and would speak very highly of him during talk show appearances promoting her upcoming acting projects (like the *X-Men* movie franchise).

Rodgers' three-year relationship with actress Olivia Munn, seen here at the Los Angeles premiere of the *LEGO Ninjago Movie*, is rumored to have caused a deep rift with his family.

Although Rodgers broke off his relationship with Munn in April of 2017, he does not appear to be moving toward reconciliation with members of his family anytime soon. During an interview with a local television station in Milwaukee, Rodgers commented about brother Jordan's new-found fame and finding love on the show, "I haven't seen the show to be honest with you, so it hasn't affected me a whole lot. I've always found it a little inappropriate to talk publicly about some family matters, so I'm just—I'm not going to speak on those things, but I wish him well in the competition."

HELPING A FRIEND

Aaron Rodgers became fast friends with Los Angeles Clippers forward and former University of Wisconsin standout basketball player Sam Dekker. Dekker, who was recently traded from the Houston Rockets to the Clippers, found himself unable to get his new kitchen garbage disposal to work in his new Los Angeles home. He called on his friend Aaron Rodgers, who lives in Los Angeles in the offseason. Turns out, all Dekker needed was a little assist from his mentor Rodgers, and to learn how to plug in his kitchen appliances.

Check out this report featuring a Twitter post from Sam Dekker showing Rodgers lending a helping hand.

GIVING BACK TO THE COMMUNITY

Since coming to Green Bay, Rodgers has been involved with various organizations and their charitable efforts. One of the largest of these organizations is the Midwest Athletes Against Childhood Cancer Fund, known locally in Wisconsin as the MAACC Fund. The MAACC Fund is responsible for raising awareness and funds for efforts toward ending the terrible disease of cancer and its devastating effect on children. His work with the MAACC Fund

A yellow ribbon is used as a symbol to raise awareness for the support of the fight against childhood cancer, a cause Rodgers actively supports.

RESEARCH PROJECT

The issue of players becoming estranged from their family is a particularly familiar one, especially for those players that have reached superstar status. Find a case within the past twenty-five years of a NFL player who cut ties with members of his family and who may or may not have reestablished those relationships while still in the league, after retiring from the game, or prior to their death or that of a loved one they were estranged from. Be sure your information discusses the nature of the strain that occurred that caused their relationship to sever, if the estrangement was permanent or reconcilable (repaired).

alone has raised more than $2 million toward the fight against childhood cancer.

Rodgers has also been involved in former Packers running back and current Offensive Coordinator Edgar Bennett's annual bowl-a-thon, as well as different celebrity golf tournaments, including the Vince Lombardi Golf Classic, a fund raiser for cancer research named after the former Green Bay Packer legendary head coach and namesake for the Super Bowl trophy given to the championship team each year.

He has taken kids in the community

Rodgers works with the Salvation Army to help end homelessness in the Green Bay area.

on shopping sprees during the holidays, and supports efforts to end homelessness and housing challenges through the Ecumenical Partnership for Housing and the Salvation Army.

One of the efforts that Aaron Rodgers is engaged in that goes largely unnoticed is his website, www.itsaaron.com. The site, launched with attorney David Gruber, was designed as an effort to highlight the accomplishments of those individuals and organizations who have made a difference in the community.

MARKETING AARON RODGERS

Aaron recently signed with the talent agency CAA Sports for representation in marketing opportunities away from the field. This includes all speaking, charitable, business, media, publishing, and other opportunities for which he is most certainly

Rodgers appeared on an episode of a sketch comedy show hosted by Keegan-Michael Key (L) and Jordan Peele in 2015.

in demand. To-date he has appeared as a contestant on (and won) *Celebrity Jeopardy*, the NBC show *The Office*, and the comedy sketch show *Key and Peele*. He is also famous for his State Farm Insurance ads, where he offers the discount double check, along with a sidekick fan, actor Adrian Martinez (who is often seen in the background of the commercial as the quarterback is talking screaming "Rodgers? Rodgers? Discount Double Check!").

Aaron Rodgers is a rare breed in the world of professional sports. His face and likeness adorn many magazine covers, and he is more than willing to publicly show his love, not only for the Green Bay Packers and game of football, but also for other sports and local teams that he has grown close to, such as the NBA Milwaukee Buck, MLB Milwaukee Brewers, and University of Wisconsin athletics. He also spends time devoted to teaching younger players at all levels the fundamentals to becoming a great quarterback and never tires from working out and continuing to work on and develop his game.

What Aaron Rodgers is not is a publicity seeker for anything that for him is either private or personal. Information about his personal relationships, family, political affiliations and preferences, and other such matters are rarely discussed by him at all. It is also rare for an athlete who has received as many awards and accolades as he has to not be constantly pitching products or lending his name to endorse many businesses (aside from the State Farm endorsements).

The future for Aaron Rodgers is certainly looking bright. He has excelled at the position of quarterback, after waiting his turn behind a Hall of Fame starter. Time will only tell just how high this star will rise and if he will be the one on top of the greatest NFL QB list when his career has finally come to a close.

#GRADTOBE

When Aaron Rodgers entered the 2005 NFL Draft, it meant he would miss his senior season at the University of California-Berkeley (Cal), and therefore fall short of graduating with a degree in American Studies. Given the outstanding success he has had in his NFL career, that decision was clearly the right choice.

Rodgers, however, has always maintained that he intends to complete his studies at Cal at some future time. He caused a stir in June of 2017 during a visit to the campus when he posted a video on Instagram with the hashtag #timetograduate. He then posted a picture of a view overlooking the campus that he hashtagged #gradtobe. The Internet being what it is, speculation was immediate that Rodgers was on campus to take summer classes (he also added #5classestilgraduation).

Rodgers quickly discounted the rumors, however, by following up with posts of himself with head football coach Justin Wilcox and other football program staffers that were accompanied by hashtags including: #goingtograduatesomeday, #notdoingsummerschoolthisyear and #thatwasajoke. Rodgers was there to visit some old friends and meet with the new football coach.

As it turns out, summer classes will be difficult for Rodgers with his current day job. Training camp for the Green Bay Packers typically conflicts with the summer class schedule at Cal.

A great believer in education and a supporter of his friends and teammates, Rodgers personally attended the graduation ceremony of Packers wide receiver Randall Cobb in 2016 in Lexington, KY. Cobb completed his degree in Community and Leadership Development from the University of Kentucky's College of Agriculture, Food and Environment, a moment the Pro Bowl receiver called his greatest accomplishment. Rodgers expressed his feelings via social media on Twitter:

"Great player, even better guy, now a college graduate. So proud of you brother."

Rodgers is too busy being one of the best quarterbacks in the NFL to finish his degree at Cal, but has said many times that he will graduate someday.

TEXT-DEPENDENT QUESTIONS:

1. On what show did the topic of Aaron Rodgers's estrangement from his family get talked about?
2. Name some of the charitable organizations that Aaron Rodgers has given his support.
3. What team traded Aaron Rodgers' friend and fellow pro athlete Sam Dekker to the Los Angeles Clippers?

blitz – a defensive strategy in which one or more linebackers or defensive backs, in addition to the defensive line, attempt to overwhelm the quarterback's protection by attacking from unexpected locations or situations.

cornerbacks – the defenders primarily responsible for preventing the offenses wide receivers from catching passes, accomplished by remaining as close to the opponent as possible during pass routes. Cornerbacks are usually the fastest players on the defense.

defensive backs – a label applied to cornerbacks and safeties, or the secondary in general.

end zone – an area 10 yards deep at either end of the field bordered by the goal line and the boundaries.

field goal – an attempt to kick the ball through the uprights, worth three points. It is taken by a specialist called the place kicker. Distances are measured from the spot of the kick plus 10 yards for the depth of the end zone.

first down – the first play in a set of four downs, or when the offense succeeds in covering 10 yards in the four downs.

fumble – when a player loses possession of the ball before being tackled, normally by contact with an opponent. Either team may recover the ball. The ground cannot cause a fumble.

goal line – the line that divides the end zones from the rest of the field. A touchdown is awarded if the ball breaks the vertical plane of the goal line while in possession or if a receiver catches the ball in the end zone.

huddle – a gathering of the offense or defense to communicate the upcoming play decided by the coach.

interception – a pass caught by a defensive player instead of an offensive receiver. The ball may be returned in the other direction.

lateral – a pass or toss behind the originating player to a teammate as measured by the lines across the field. Although the offense may only make one forward pass per play, there is no limit to the number of laterals at any time.

line of scrimmage – an imaginary line, determined by the ball's location before each play, that extends across the field from sideline to sideline. Seven offensive players must be on the line of scrimmage, though the defense can set up in any formation. Forward passes cannot be thrown from beyond the line of scrimmage.

pass – when the ball is thrown to a receiver who is farther down the field. A team is limited to one such forward pass per play. Normally this is the duty of the quarterback, although technically any eligible receiver can pass the ball.

play action – a type of offensive play in which the quarterback pretends to hand the ball to a running back before passing the ball. The goal is to fool the secondary into weakening their pass coverage.

play clock – visible behind the end zone at either end of the stadium. Once a play is concluded, the offense has 40 seconds to snap the ball for the next play. The duration is reduced to 25 seconds for game-related stoppages such as penalties. Time is kept on the play clock. If the offense does not snap the ball before the play clock elapses, they incur a 5-yard penalty for delay of game.

punt – a kick, taken by a special teams player called the punter, that surrenders possession to the opposing team. This is normally done on fourth down when the offense deems gaining a first down unlikely.

receiver – an offensive player who may legally catch a pass, almost always wide receivers, tight ends, and running backs. Only the two outermost players on either end of the line of scrimmage—even wide receivers who line up distantly from the offensive line—or the four players behind the line of scrimmage (such as running backs, another wide receiver, and the quarterback) are eligible receivers. If an offensive lineman, normally an ineligible receiver, is placed on the outside of the line of scrimmage because of an unusual formation, he is considered eligible but must indicate his eligibility to game officials before the play.

run – a type of offensive play in which the quarterback, after accepting the ball from center, either keeps it and heads upfield or gives the ball to another player, who then attempts to move ahead with the help of blocking teammates.

sack – a play in which the defense tackles the quarterback behind the line of scrimmage on a pass play.

safety – 1) the most uncommon scoring play in football. When an offensive player is tackled in his own end zone, the defensive team is awarded two points and receives the ball via a kick; 2) a defensive secondary position divided into two roles, free safety and strong safety.

snap – the action that begins each play. The center must snap the ball between his legs, usually to the quarterback, who accepts the ball while immediately behind the center or several yards farther back in a formation called the shotgun.

special teams – the personnel that take the field for the punts, kickoffs, and field goals, or a generic term for that part of the game.

tackle – 1) a term for both an offensive and defensive player. The offensive tackles line up on the outside of the line, but inside the tight end, while the defensive tackles protect the interior of their line; 2) the act of forcing a ball carrier to touch the ground with any body part other than the hand or feet. This concludes a play.

tight end – an offensive player who normally lines up on the outside of either offensive tackle. Multiple tight ends are frequently employed on running plays where the offense requires only a modest gain. Roles vary between blocking or running pass routes.

touchdown – scored when the ball breaks the vertical plane of the goal line. Worth six points and the scoring team can add a single additional point by kick or two points by converting from the 2-yard line with an offensive play.

FURTHER READING

Challen, Paul. *What Does a Quarterback Do?* New York: The Rosen Publishing Group, 2015.

Crepeau, Richard C. *NFL Football: A History of America's New National Pastime*. Urbana, IL: University of Illinois Press, 2014.

Editors of Sports Illustrated. *Sports Illustrated NFL QB: The Greatest Position in Sports*. New York: Time Home Entertainment, 2014.

Feldman, Bruce. *The QB: The Making of Modern Quarterbacks*. New York: Three Rivers Press, 2014.

Hailey, Ron. *Aaron Rodgers: A Biography*. North Charleston: CreateSpace Independent Publishing Platform, 2017.

Morey, Allan. Morey, Allan. *The Green Bay Packers Story*. Minneapolis, MN: Torque Books, 2016.

Schatz, Aaron, Mike Tanier, Sterling Xie, and Vincent Verhei. *Football Outsiders Almanac 2016: The Essential Guide to the 2016 NFL and College Football Seasons*. North Charleston: CreateSpace Independent Publishing Platform, 2016.

Wilner, Barry and Ken Rappoport. *On the Clock: The Story of the NFL Draft*. Lanham: Taylor Trade Publishing, 2015.

INTERNET RESOURCES

http://bleacherreport.com/nfl
The official website for Bleacher Report Sport's NFL reports on each of the thirty-two teams.

https://www.cbssports.com/nfl/teams/page/GB/green-bay-packers
The web page for the Green Bay Packers provided by CBSSports.com, providing latest news and information, player profiles, scheduling, and standings.

http://www.greenbaypackers.com
The official website for the Green Bay Packers football club, including history, player information, statistics, and news.

www.espn.com/
The official website of ESPN sports network.

http://www.footballdb.com/teams/nfl/greenbay-packers/history
The Football Database, a reputable news source, Green Bay Packers web page providing historical rosters, results, statistics, and draft information.

www.nfl.com/
The official website of the National Football League.

www.pro-football-reference.com/
The football specific resource provided by Sports Reference LLC for current and historical statistics of players, teams, scores, and leaders in the NFL, AFL, and AAFC.

https://sports.yahoo.com/nfl/
The official website of Yahoo! Sports NFL coverage, providing news, statistics, and important information about the league and the thirty-two teams.

INDEX

Chapter 1

© Scott Anderson | Dreamstime

© Scott Anderson | Dreamstime

© Jerry Coli | Dreamstime

Chapter 2

© Scott Anderson | Dreamstime

© Aspenphoto | Dreamstime

© Darwin Lopez | Dreamstime

Wiki Commons – Mike Morbeck

© Scott Anderson | Dreamstime

Lance Cpl. Matthew Bragg

Chapter 3

© Scott Anderson | Dreamstime

© Jerry Coli | Dreamstime

© Jerry Coli | Dreamstime

© Jerry Coli | Dreamstime

Chapter 4

© Scott Anderson | Dreamstime

© Jerry Coli | Dreamstime

© Allison14 | Dreamstime

Wiki Commons

© Scott Anderson | Dreamstime

© Jenta Wong | Dreamstime

Chapter 5

© Jerry Coli | Dreamstime

© Starstock | Dreamstime

© Oleksandr Bilyi | Dreamstime

© Ignisign | Dreamstime

© Dwong19 | Dreamstime

© Jerry Coli | Dreamstime.com

EDUCATIONAL VIDEO LINKS

CHAPTER 1

http://x-qr.net/1Dac

http://x-qr.net/1FpL

http://x-qr.net/1HHf

http://x-qr.net/1Eux

http://x-qr.net/1GML

http://x-qr.net/1Fw1

http://x-qr.net/1E5A

http://x-qr.net/1Fg9

CHAPTER 2

http://x-qr.net/1DtN

CHAPTER 3

http://x-qr.net/1HBG

http://x-qr.net/1H6d

CHAPTER 4

http://x-qr.net/1F3g

CHAPTER 5

http://x-qr.net/1HET

ABOUT THE AUTHOR

Joe L. Morgan is a father, author, and an avid sports fan. He enjoys every type of professional sport, including NFL, NBA, MLB, and European club soccer. He enjoyed a brief career as a punter and a defensive back at the NCAA Division III level, and now spends much of his time watching and writing about the sports he loves.